PENGUINS

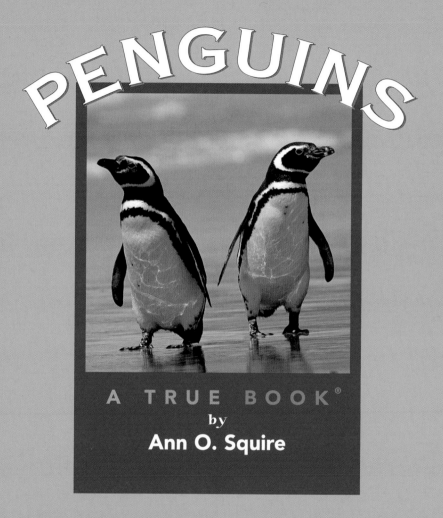

A TRUE BOOK®

by

Ann O. Squire

Children's Press®
A Division of Scholastic Inc.

New York Toronto London Auckland Sydney
Mexico City New Delhi Hong Kong
Danbury, Connecticut

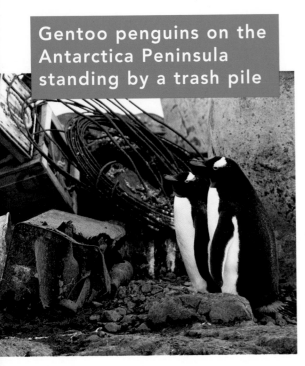

Gentoo penguins on the Antarctica Peninsula standing by a trash pile

Content Consultant
Kathy Carlstead, PhD
Research Scientist
Honolulu Zoo

Reading Consultant
Cecilia Minden-Cupp, PhD
Former Director, Language and Literacy Program
Harvard Graduate School of Education

Author's Dedication
For Emma

The photograph on the cover shows two emperor penguins and their chick at Antarctica's Atka Bay. The photograph on the title page shows two Magellanic penguins.

Library of Congress Cataloging-in-Publication Data
Squire, Ann.
    Penguins / by Ann O. Squire.
        p. cm. — (A True Book)
    Includes bibliographical references and index.
    ISBN-10: 0-516-25472-3 (lib. bdg.)   0-516-25583-5 (pbk.)
    ISBN-13: 978-0-516-25472-2 (lib. bdg.)   978-0-516-25583-5 (pbk.)
    1. Penguins—Juvenile literature. I. Title. II. Series.
QL696.S473S69 2006
598.47—dc22   2005003634

CHILDREN'S PRESS, and A TRUE BOOK™, and associated logos are trademarks and/or registered trademarks of Scholastic Library Publishing. SCHOLASTIC and associated logos are trademarks and/or registered trademarks of Scholastic Inc.
1 2 3 4 5 6 7 8 9 10 R 16 15 14 13 12 11 10 09 08 07

Contents

Adélie penguins dive off an iceberg.

A Bird That Doesn't Fly

If you've ever watched penguins swoop through the water or dive off icy cliffs, you may have trouble believing that these graceful creatures are actually birds. Like other birds, penguins have wings and beaks. Their bodies are covered with feathers. Like other birds, penguins lay eggs.

But unlike other birds, penguins cannot fly through the air. They "fly" underwater instead. Penguins use their small wings to paddle. They use their tails, wings, and feet to steer.

The earliest penguins were flying birds. Over time, they adapted to life in the ocean. They traded the ability to fly for the ability to swim and dive. Their large wings, which would have been

Like all penguins, the gentoo penguin has small wings.

useless underwater, became smaller and stiffer.

A long, sleek body helps the penguin move quickly underwater.

The penguins developed short, dense feathers that act as a waterproof wet suit. Their bones got heavier. Their bodies took on a long, sleek shape.

All these changes made it easier for penguins to live in the water. But the penguins looked less and less like other birds.

Today, there are seventeen kinds, or **species**, of penguins. The smallest are fairy penguins. They stand about 15 inches (38 centimeters) tall and weigh about 2 pounds (.9 kilograms). The biggest are emperor penguins. They can reach 4 feet (1.2 m) in height and weigh up to 90 pounds (41 kg).

All seventeen penguin species live in the Southern Hemisphere. The Southern Hemisphere is the half of Earth that is south of the **equator**, an imaginary line around Earth's middle.

Only two species, the Adélie penguin and the emperor penguin, live on the frozen land of Antarctica. Most penguins live farther north, in New Zealand or along the coast of South America.

Another species, the Galápagos penguin, lives on islands just

Adélie penguins
(top) and emperor
penguins (bottom)
live on the Antarctic
mainland.

The Galápagos penguin lives on the Galápagos Islands off the coast of Ecuador.

south of the equator. The Galápagos penguin lives farther north than any other penguin.

Penguins tend to live on land with few or no animals to hunt them. The penguins' inability to fly makes them easy targets for **predators** on land.

Because penguins cannot fly, they are easy for land predators to hunt.

Life in the Cold

Penguins are truly waterbirds. Some species spend months in the ocean without returning to land. Penguins have even been spotted with small shell-fish called **barnacles** growing on their tails. This is a sure sign that they have been at sea for a long time.

A Humboldt penguin swims in the ocean.

An emperor penguin jumps out of the icy seawater.

Penguins live in the world's coldest ocean currents. They need special ways of staying warm. Like seals and whales, penguins have a thick layer of fat that protects them from the icy water. Penguins in colder climates are often fatter than penguins in warmer climates.

The penguin's feathers also help the bird survive the cold. The tiny feathers are packed tightly. They overlap at the tips to form a waterproof coat.

Beneath these outer feathers are soft, fluffy feathers called **down** that trap air next to the skin. They work to keep the bird warm, just like the filling of a down jacket.

The penguin often cleans and smooths its feathers, or **preens**. The penguin uses its beak to pick up oil from the base of its tail. Then the penguin spreads the oil over its feathers. The oil helps the feathers repel water.

A king penguin uses its beak to preen its lower feathers.

Even its black and white coloring helps the penguin stay warm. When the sun shines down on the penguin's back, the black feathers absorb the heat. That raises the bird's body temperature.

Penguins are so well suited to life in the cold ocean that they have a problem when they come ashore. Sometimes they get too hot!

To keep from overheating, penguins pant like dogs to

Flapping its flippers helps
this African penguin cool off.

cool off. They also ruffle their
feathers and hold their wings
away from their bodies
to get rid of extra heat.

Penguins on Land

All penguins are at home in the water. Some species spend as much as three-quarters of their time out at sea. They search for fish and squid. They also look for **crustaceans**, such as the tiny, shrimplike krill.

With an ocean full of food, why would a penguin ever

Penguins cannot molt or breed in the sea. They must return to land.

return to land? There are two important reasons: **molting** and breeding.

It's Black and White

Do you know why penguins are black on the back and white on the front? One reason is that their unusual coloring helps them hide from enemies. To predators looking down from above, the black back blends into the dark ocean. To predators looking up from underwater, the penguin's white belly disappears against the light sky.

An emperor penguin

Like other birds, penguins shed their worn-out feathers and grow new ones each year. This process is called molting. For many birds, molting happens slowly. It may even be hard to notice that they are molting.

Molting is a big problem for penguins, however. When they lose their feathers, they also lose their waterproof protection. They cannot go in the water to feed until new feathers have grown in.

Before molting, penguins swim out to sea and eat as much as they can. When they return to land, they are so fat that they can barely waddle up onto the shore. Then they wait.

Soon the penguins' old feathers start falling out in clumps. Molting may take weeks. During that time, the penguins do not eat at all. By the time their new feathers have grown in, the birds have lost half their body weight.

During the molting process, new feathers replace old.

Penguins also come ashore to find a mate, build a nest, and raise chicks. Penguins are social birds, and most species build their nests in very crowded conditions.

A group, or colony, of breeding penguins may number in the thousands or even in the millions. As many as four penguins may nest in a space only slightly larger than the mat outside your front door.

Penguins often breed in huge colonies.

Chinstrap penguins spread their wings and call to the females.

A penguin colony is also very noisy. After finding a spot to make a nest, the male penguin stands up tall and spreads his wings. He makes a variety of squeaks, squawks, and calls.

By communicating in this way, the male penguin is letting other males know that this tiny piece of land is his own. He is also signaling to female penguins that he is looking for a mate.

Raising Chicks

After the male and female have gotten together, they continue to call and bow to each other as they build their nest. Different penguin species have different ways of attracting each other. King penguins sing long songs with their partners. Gentoo penguin males often give their mates gifts of small stones.

For penguins, bonding is an important part of raising a chick.

These behaviors are important. They help the male and female form a close bond. It takes two parents working together to raise even one chick successfully.

Penguin nests are usually simple. Adélie and chinstrap penguins build nests of small stones. Gentoo penguins use stones, feathers, and grasses. Fairy penguins nest in burrows. Most penguin species lay two eggs.

Emperor and king penguins, the two largest species, build no nests at all and lay a single egg. They warm or **incubate** the egg on their feet and cover it with a flap of skin.

A chinstrap penguin examines its eggs (top). A king penguin incubates its single egg (bottom).

The parents take turns incubating the egg or eggs. The female feeds at sea while the male tends to the eggs. On her return, the hungry male leaves to find food.

The eggs hatch after about one or two months. Tiny, down-covered chicks emerge. Their soft, fluffy feathers are not waterproof, so the chicks must stay out of the ocean. They wait for their parents to bring them food.

The chicks need their parents to keep them warm. They depend totally on their mother and father until waterproof feathers replace their fluffy down coats. When that finally happens, the chicks go to sea and find food on their own.

Problems for Penguins

Penguins face many dangers, on land or at sea. They are likely to meet predators such as leopard seals, sea lions, and killer whales at sea. On shore, foxes, snakes, rats, or dogs attack penguins. Seabirds such as skuas, sheathbills, and gulls eat penguin eggs and chicks.

Killer whales hunt penguins on the sea ice in Antarctica.

In the past, people ate penguin eggs. They also hunted adult penguins for their feathers and skin. Oil from the birds' fat layers was used as fuel.

People even scooped up penguin droppings, called **guano**. They used it to fertilize soil to help grow crops.

How could that possibly have harmed penguins? The answer is that some penguin species make their nests in thick layers of guano. When the guano was scraped away, the birds had to lay their eggs on the bare ground, where predators were more likely to eat them.

African penguins are covered with oil from a tanker spill.

Today's penguins face other dangers, too. Those dangers include oil spills and other changes in the birds' surroundings. Sometimes penguins don't find enough to eat because the fishing industry has caught too many fish.

Even the weather can affect penguins. Gradual warming of Earth's climate reduces the amount of sea ice. It also affects the penguins' food supply.

Can the world's penguins be saved? No one knows for sure. You can help by learning all you can about penguins and the organizations that work to protect these fascinating birds.

Adélie penguins walk across a snowfield as they return from the sea.

To Find Out More

Here are some additional resources to help you learn more about penguins:

 **Books**

Jacquet, Luc. **March of the Penguins**. National Geographic Children's Books, 2005.

Lynch, Wayne. **Penguins!** Firefly Books, 1999.

Swan, Erin Pembrey. **Penguins: From Emperors to Macaronis**. Franklin Watts, 2003.

Swanson, Diane. **Penguins**. Gareth Stevens, 2004.

Taylor, Barbara. **Penguins**. Lorenz Books, 2004.

Webb, Sophie. **My Season with Penguins: An Antarctic Journal**. Houghton Mifflin Company, 2000.

Winner, Cherie. **Penguins**. NorthWord Press, 2002.

Organizations and Online Sites

Emperor Penguins

http://www.nationalgeographic
.com/kids/creature_feature
/0101/penguins.html

This National Geographic Society site includes fun facts and a video about emperors, the largest penguin species.

International Penguin Conservation Work Group

Casilla 263
Punta Arenas
Chile
http://www.penguins.cl/

This conservation group was formed in 2000 to address threats to penguin populations worldwide. The site has information about penguins by region and species.

New England Aquarium

Central Wharf
Boston, MA 02110
617-973-5200
http://www.neaq.org/penguins

The New England Aquarium has one of the largest and most successful penguin colonies in North America. Check out individual penguin species pages as well as information about visiting the aquarium.

New Zealand Penguins

http://www.penguin.net.nz/

This New Zealand–based site features frequently asked questions with accompanying photographs, conservation information, games, and two penguin webcams.

San Francisco Zoo

1 Zoo Road
San Francisco, CA 94132
415-753-7080
http://www.sfzoo.org/
cgi-bin/animals.py?ID=54

The San Francisco Zoo has one of the most successful breeding colonies of Magellanic penguins in a zoo. Check out the site for fascinating facts and photos as well as visitor information.

Important Words

barnacles small crustaceans that attach themselves to rocks, whales, or boats

crustaceans sea animals with a skeleton on the outside, such as crabs and krill

down soft, fluffy feathers

equator an imaginary line around the middle of Earth

guano droppings of seabirds

incubate to hatch eggs using body heat

molting the process in which birds shed their feathers and grow new ones

predators animals that hunt and eat other animals

preen to clean and smooth the feathers

species a group of animals that have similar characteristics and a common name

Index

Meet the Author

Ann O. Squire has a PhD in animal behavior. Before becoming a writer, she spent several years studying African electric fish and the special signals they use to communicate with each other. Dr. Squire is the author of many books on natural science and animals, including *Beluga Whales*, *Lemmings*, *Moose*, *Polar Bears*, and *Puffins*. She lives with her family in Katonah, New York.